BALTIMORE
DECO

An Architectural Survey
of Art Deco in Baltimore
By S. Cucchiella

Photographs by John Kardys and others

Maclay & Associates, Inc.
Baltimore, 1984

To Leona Rosen
My Grandmother

C O N T E N T S

INTRODUCTION

Art Deco has been aptly described as the "last complete style." This is because architects and craftsmen applied the newest design principles to each project that crossed their drawing boards. We see Deco influence in the jewelry, clothing, furniture, appliances, and transportation vehicles of the era that occurred between the world wars. The style was also in harmony with fine arts and music, as expressed in the cubist movement and jazz rhythms of the time. There was a general feeling of liberation from the rigidity of classical styles and the heaviness of Victorian design. Prompted by a grasping toward "newness" and an identification with the 20th century, modernism developed. At first the Art Deco style was confused, but exhibitions such as the "International Exhibition of Modern Decorative and Industrial Arts," held in Paris in 1925, helped to unify it. Incorporated as basic elements in the overall design were Egyptian and Aztec motifs. Influence from the Russian ballet and the Orient contributed to the further development and incorporation of romantic themes into the Deco style. The most noted examples of this fusion of styles are the designs for the ocean liners **Normandie** and **Ile de France.**

Art Deco, though sometimes characterized as lavish and ornate, could also be simple, linear, and geometric. This diversity of elements and motifs is exemplified by the apparent unity common to a lavish Jean Harlow movie set and an austere interior by Le Corbusier: a unity based on one of the most fundamental changes in the history of style—the final and total acceptance of the machine. America embraced the machine age with enthusiasm and this was reflected in the architecture of the era. Not only were automobiles and locomotives beginning to look more streamlined, but so too were buildings. Important to the movement toward streamlining was the added emphasis on technological function. Repetitive geometric design and the use of the latest finish materials, such as chrome, stainless steel, and colored mirror, became basic to Art Deco style in America. Glass block, imported from Holland, also became a prime element in architectural design. The lavishness of the 1920s Art Deco style, although not as popular in this country as in Europe, is most evident in monumental buildings such as New York's Chrysler building and Radio City Music Hall.

Although the depression of 1929 pushed the United States toward artistic independence from European standards, there was still an undeniable European influence on American design. In 1929 the Metropolitan Museum of Art held an exhibition entitled "The Architect and the International Arts," directed by Fliel Saarinen. This was an attempt to combine European design with America's changing needs. Direct European influence came about in the United States when prominent designers fled their native countries to escape Fascism and Nazism. As the economy began to recover, the United States experienced mechanical progress as well. In 1934 the Metropolitan Museum of Art held another "Exhibition of Industrial Art," which celebrated modernism and provided a framework for the 1939 New York World's Fair.

Baltimore Deco has a distinctive style with few of the elements of the lavish 1920s. The Maryland National Bank building, built in 1929, is one of the more ornate exceptions. The tallest building in the city when it opened, it is also noteworthy in that it represented the craftsmanship of Baltimoreans. The Hutzler building on Howard Street can also be classified as exceptional in reference to Baltimore Art Deco. This streamlined structure is reminiscent of a New York skyscraper, complete with an outstanding interior. Another example of a commercial Art Deco interior is Werner's, a small luncheonette on Redwood Street. Intact are the booths, wall decoration and stainless steel embellished counter. The Community Service Center of City

Hospitals, on Eastern Avenue, features a pair of Sphinx-like structures flanking the entry. This building was considered controversial when built because of the contrast it had with the rest of the complex. Located near the City Hospitals building is the Circle Drive-In—one of the city's best examples of architectural kitsch. Baltimore's premier theater, the Senator, reminds us of the era in which theatergoing was a total experience, a marriage of architecture and art.

Baltimore Deco is best described as a sampling of Deco elements, applied when function demanded their use. Deco buildings are found throughout the city, scattered amid such famous Baltimore jewels as the Georgian rowhouses and Gothic Revival churches. Few Art Deco buildings were built in Baltimore in the years between the wars. The style developed here later and many Deco buildings were actually built in the late 1940s, which makes it impossible to assign definite dates to the Baltimore Deco period. The buildings mentioned here are by no means all of the fine examples of Art Deco architecture and ornament in our city, and it is to be hoped that they will remain a source of pride to our community. Unfortunately, some have already felt the toll of ''rehabilitation,'' but with increased public awareness of the period, sensitive restoration can be accomplished.

ACKNOWLEDGEMENTS

I wish to thank all those who helped me with this project, and am grateful to many friends who provided support and guidance. A heartfelt and special thanks is reserved for Mary Cowgill, without whose assistance this book could not have been written. Thanks also to Jacques Kelly for his interest; the Senator Theater; Donald Sherman (formerly of the Maryland Institute of Art); and the photographers who made their work available to me.

Designed by Mary Pat Andrea
Produced by John Maclay

BALTIMORE
DECO

COMMERCIAL

**Hutzler Brothers
Department Store**
212 North Howard Street
1932
J. Edmunds, Jr., Architect

Hutzler's is one of the most important Art Deco buildings in Baltimore. The **Moderne** skyscraper is architecturally unique to our area. On the exterior, red brick is used for vertical direction in the design and black glazed brick is used as a horizontal divider between window levels. The overall effect is sleekly geometric.

On the corners of the building, "Hutzler's" appears on inset concrete vertical bands. Under the signage is one large faceted window which has bullnose fluted columns on either side. This is an excellent example of one of Art Deco's fundamental designs— always an attempt to play the geometric elements against each other.

The exterior of the first story is made of polished black granite with a stepped-in pediment over each entry area. Over this pediment is etched the store name and date, and an oval medallion in **Moderne** typeface. A continuous horizontal cornice goes the entire length of the building and supports two large carved urns which have recessed lighting fixtures and are placed in front, on the faceted windows. Geometrically-divided display windows are important in the pedestrian level design. The bronze screens which were fabricated for these windows have unfortunately been removed to another location.

The recessed entry features a beautiful pair of revolving brass and glass doors. Above them the bowed striped transoms are edged in decorative molding. Important Deco symbols, the caduceus, fins, and sunrise motifs, are located on the front exterior.

The interior is noteworthy and exemplifies store design of the era.

Note: Luncheonette closed in 1984.

Window Dressing
January, 1947

Window Dressing   Interior
September, 1947   c. 1950

Maryland National Bank
Baltimore & Light Streets
1929
Taylor & Fisher,
Smith & May, Architects

This building won an architectural medal in 1929 for design excellence and was regarded as Baltimore's first major example of skyscraper architecture. It represented the work of **Baltimoreans**—artisans, architects, artists, bricklayers and others.

The use of symbols as ornamentation is important. References to Mayan culture are evident, although modified. There are symbols representing Baltimore's history as well.

The shipping and railroad industries, the writing of ''The Star Spangled Banner,'' and many other events are pictured in sculptural relief.

The building is 500 feet tall and 192 feet long. It has 34 stories of brick structure which are built onto a five-story Indiana limestone base. On top of the stone cornice at the fifth-floor level, a frieze extends around the building. The whole structure was built in a series of setbacks (in accordance with zoning ordinances of the time) which climaxes in a copper-roofed tower. The addition of the ''MN'' signage occurred in 1971. The tower was originally spotlighted and could be seen from all over the city. The entrance arches are rich with sculptural ornamentation and direct one into the lavish interior.

Commercial Credit Company
301 North Charles Street
1930
Mottu & White, Architects

This limestone monumental
building features a massive arched
entry area with intricately-carved
brass Deco grating. An etched
scene portraying Baltimore's
history is part of the metal
transom detail. Above the entry is
a band of carved relief that frames
the company name. Vertically-
oriented applied details separate
the window bays which consist of
three windows each. The two
shorter towers of the structure
have one bay and the tall middle
section, which is recessed above
the relief, contains three bays.
Street-level display windows have
brass Deco moldings with sunrise
motifs and marble inlay panels.
The rich use of materials and
symbolism makes this building an
important example of Baltimore
Deco.

C & P Telephone Company
320 St. Paul Street
1941
Taylor & Fisher, Architects

This skyscraper is built of white granite and buff limestone. The severe, simple exterior lines are vertically-oriented as is evident in the vertical stone piers which separate the windows and the setback three-story entry. A horizontal rhythm is created with the use of black stone panels to divide the window levels above the monumental stainless steel entry. Black stone is similarly used at the second-story level but the panels are carved with Deco motifs. Stainless steel is also used as decorative border for the windows at the street level.

First Federal Savings & Loan
3401 Greenmount Avenue
1938
F. Thomas, Architect

A rounded wraparound corner emphasizes the streamlined effect of this buff brick and granite building. The upper portion features a black glazed brick ribbon and a glass block curved corner window. Steel casement windows echo the faceted look of the glass block. The bullnose brick at the window openings complements the curve of the overall design.

First National Bank
3401 Eastern Avenue
1940
J.F. Eyring, Architect

This sleek concrete block building has stepped-in fluted corners and curved polished terrazzo foundation molding. The two-story entry surround is of stainless steel as is the Deco cornice molding, on top of which is a geometrically-divided transom. Two metal and opal glass light fixtures are mounted on either side of the entry.

Commercial Building
1020 St. Paul Street
1938
Palmer & Lamdin, Architects

This two-story stucco building with steel casement windows has a sleek, flowing form which is enhanced by simple trim and molding. The continuous ribbon molding at the top of the first story sets the horizontal rhythm for the bullnose window detail, which parallels the curve at the entry. The striping of stucco between windows lines up with the mullions of the windows to complete the geometric pattern. Fluted columns frame the entry and an arched iron handrail again repeats the curved element.

Commercial Building
930 North Charles Street
1932
Architect unknown

A granite front with black metal strips inserted into channels cut to form an angled pattern provides a sleek exterior for this structure. The **Moderne** appearance is heightened by shiny black glass street numbers, and display windows trimmed in stainless steel. Stepped-back black granite stairs leading to the entrance, which is surrounded by angled walls, complete the design.

Hochschild Kohn & Company
Belvedere Avenue & York Road
1949
James R. Edmunds, Jr., Architect

Built of buff-colored brick, this
building sweeps around the corner
of Belvedere and York Road with
all the style and elegance of the
earliest Deco buildings.
This solid structure is windowless
except for the street-level display
windows (now bricked in). The
curve is important in the design
statement; there is a curved
"showcase" corner, which runs
almost full height, composed of
faceted glass panels and stainless
steel trim. A circular revolving
stainless steel door leads into the
entry area which features a wind-
ing aluminum-railed stairway. This
elegant store contains 45,000
square feet of sales floor space.
The interior will undergo restoration in 1984.

Kresge's
119 West Lexington Street
1937
Emile Jehle, Architect

A very streamlined **Moderne** look
dominates this three-story structure which occupies and curves
around a corner site with the style
of a locomotive of the era. The
play of continuous horizontal
elements against vertical elements
sets the dramatic rhythm of the
design. Flat stone pilasters separate
the plate glass display windows of
the first story. Over the first story
cornice is a frieze sheathed in red-
painted metal. Above this is an area
of glass block over which "Kresge's"
is spelled out in yellow letters. The
second and third-story windows are
separated in groups by two-story
fluted vertical pilasters and a green
stone horizontally-striped panel
separates the window level of each
floor.

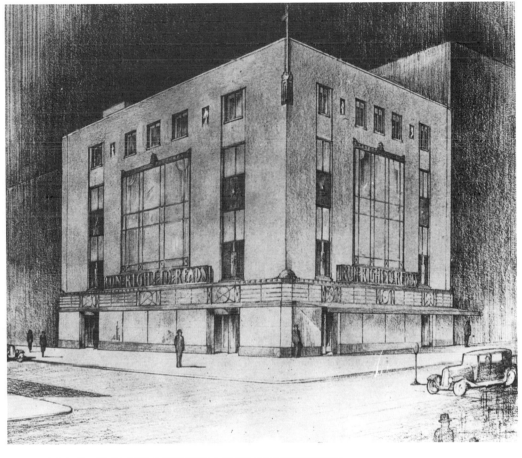

Read's Drug Store
Howard & Lexington Streets

The original Read's building had fine Deco railings, lettering, and two-story steel windows. Few of these features remain today as the building has been insensitively renovated.

Greenspring Dairy
1020 West 41st Street
1937
Lucius White, Architect

The Dairy has a buff brick exterior
and decorative stepped-back brick
is used as an effective accent
detail. Glass block has been used
extensively on the main building
and central tower section of the
entry. The tower contains a vertical glass block stripe which accentuates the strong linear design element and breaks up the sprawling
horizontal mass of the factory
building. Of note is the stainless
steel signage over the entry, which
is a good example of Art Deco
lettering.

Fiske Catering
411-413 West Cold Spring Lane
1933
Lucius White, Architect

The exterior finish on this structure is buff-colored, pebble-
encrusted concrete with black and
red Aztec-inspired geometric
motifs. The building is of simple
design with a central continuous
horizontal ribbon that is in-
tersected by vertical striping, upon
which rests the original signage,
displaying the typical lettering style
of the period. Stainless steel
display window molding and a
lower-level entry complement the
overall design statement.

Werner's
223 Redwood Street

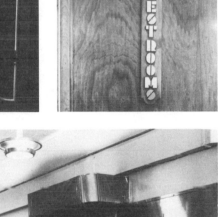

Chesapeake Cadillac
2401 North Charles Street
1930
Howard F. Baldwin, Architect

This car dealership opened on March 15, 1930 as Cunliffe Cadillac Company; today it is still being used for its original purpose by Chesapeake Cadillac, and remains in excellent condition. It is constructed of granite block; the overall appearance is that of a solid mass which incorporates geometric elements into the design. The faceted steel casement windows are separated by two-story vertical piers. At street level, there are display windows with a segmented ribbon transom that echoes the facets above. The entry is surrounded by carved molding that has "Cadillac" engraved over the canopied doorway. Of special interest are the carved stone eagles which rest on each corner of the building. The interior underwent renovation in 1983.

Michael's Rug Gallery
415-417 33rd Street
1936
Benjamin Frank, Architect

Geometric Art Deco designs etched in polished black granite are a beautiful and unusual feature of the building's facade. The exterior above the granite consists of buff brick within which is a horizontal concrete stripe. Strong vertical elements frame the set-back entrance and right corner of the building. A concrete finial in skyscraper style tops these elements, and a diagonal pattern of brick ribbons across the top of the building.

Schwing Motors
3326 Keswick Road
1948
F.J. Heldrich, Architect

This unusual building has a streamlined curved front reminiscent of an ocean liner. The effect is enhanced by a curved wall of glass which has a band of glass block at the top. Above this is a continuous solid stripe of stucco on which the company name is displayed. Solid vertical planes of stucco intersect the glass and second story to add to the rhythmic architecture. Note: The building facade was altered in 1982.

Alonso's
415 West Cold Spring Lane
1945
W. Schaeffer, Contractor

Alonso's Bar has two unusual
features consistent with Deco era
design. The bar itself is made of
stainless steel and is the only one
known in the United States. The
facade is also stainless steel and
believed to be the only one in the
country.

Hippo
934-936 North Charles Street
1939
John Poe Tyler, Architect

This red brick wraparound front
corner building with its striped
stucco upper portion is notable for
its geometric styling. The use of a
cylindric shape which has fluted
metal trim adds to the streamlined
effect. A globe finial, upon which
used to rest a large rooster, still
remains as a crown for the main
entry. This building has always
been in use as a nightclub and bar.

Club Charles
1724 North Charles Street

The Salvage Depot
2801 Sisson Street

White Tower
Erdman Avenue & Belair Road
Howard & Centre Streets
1945, 1948
Architect unknown

The White Tower chain started in 1926 and was open 24 hours a day, seven days a week. The original theme for the restaurants was medieval, but variations began almost as soon as the idea was conceived. As demand for the structures grew, they were produced in an almost assembly-line manner, and standardization of the design became important to the chain's goal of expansion. In the 1930s the White Tower chain used many important Deco finish materials such as Vitrolite, stainless steel, glass block, and terra cotta.

There was a deliberate design relationship between the interior and exterior. Strong geometric elements were emphasized by the vertical tower which had stepped-in molding. Bullnosed or rounded corners were used when possible, as was curved window glass.

However, when the chain's budget had to be tightened, buildings became more streamlined and the interiors became more efficient. The "look" of the White Tower chain, although formed and refined during the Deco years, remained a construction standard well into the 1950s. Only two White Towers of this design style remain in Baltimore. The White Tower signage on the Howard Street store was the original design for the logo which is still used by the company today.

Buttercrisp Bakery
3215 Greenmount Avenue
1937
Architect unknown

The buff brick exterior of this structure has vertical and horizontal stripes of black glazed brick and features several striking Art Deco elements. The storefront is two-toned enamel with an arched opening framing the bowed display windows. Blue mirrored glass trims either side of the doorway and the round display window. Stainless steel is used in the lettering above the window and also as an exterior trim material. The concrete cornice has vertical accents that mimic the geometric design of the brick.
The bakery's interior features the original baked goods cases with stepped-in geometric styling, rounded edges, and Deco lettering.

The Circle Drive-In
555 Dundalk Avenue
Date unknown
Architect unknown

This building is one of Baltimore's finest examples of playful architecture. The round white stucco exterior is divided horizontally by a red brick ribbon. It also features glass block inserts and stainless steel canopies. The prominent rooftop bulb sign of a hamburger is the major advertising element used, other than a small "circle" in stucco over the entrance. Their speciality, which is Bar-B-Q, is spelled out in large letters which are bulb-lit as well.

**General Vending
Sales Corporation**
237-245 West Biddle Street
1946
Hal A. Miller, Architect

This red and buff brick structure
has an overall sculptured look and
was designed for its present use.
The use of curved corners with
glass block inserts adds a direc-
tional accent and gives the structure a very streamlined and sleek-
faced appearance. A concrete
eyebrow molding runs down the
exterior from the rooftop sign and
bisects the building horizontally to
provide geometric rhythm. This is
interrupted by a concrete block
entry which runs the full height of
the building and features fluted
bullnose columns framing stainless
steel doors. The doors have
round window openings with
decorative steel rail pulls in a
geometric pattern. The area of
the building where red brick is
used has stepped-back symmet-
rical patterns.

General Vending
Sales Corporation
Recessed Cathode Ray Lighting

Greyhound Bus Terminal
Howard & Centre Streets
1941
Architect unknown

This building is constructed of buff concrete with black brick and stone accents. It was built to be a transit terminal and the design elements suggest this end use. The stepped-down side facades, along with the interplay of horizontal and vertical detailing, suggest a fluid, sleek movement. The aluminum windows travel horizontally as the building curves around the corner site. In 1941, the Greyhound Bus Terminal won an award for design excellence.

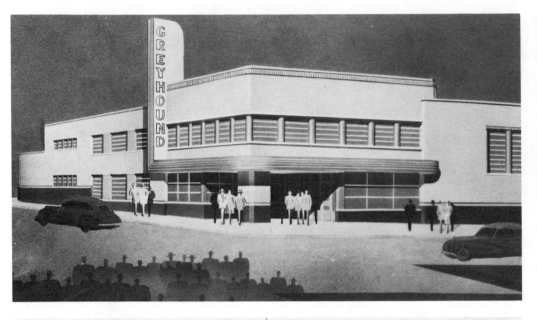

BALTIMORE
DECO

HOLLYWOOD

THEATERS

Even though most of our Deco movie houses have been closed down or altered for other uses, a few still remain in operation. These are a pleasure to behold. Theater architecture during the Deco years tended to draw the viewer inside through the overall design and the use of flashy finish materials. The newest and finest materials of the era can be found again and again—glass block, stainless steel, and of course, neon. These sculptural, geometric buildings were designed for the pleasure, escape, and enjoyment of the movie-going public. The movie industry prospered in the 20s and 30s and theaters payed homage to this success. The use of interior murals, statuary, and tapestries created an environment of fantasy in harmony with the fantasies portrayed on the screen.

Theater attendance vastly diminished with the advent of television in the 50s. These grand old buildings became too costly to maintain and many gradually declined. Some were recycled and put to different uses; others were demolished to make room for new structures.

Ambassador
4604 Liberty Heights Road
1935
John Zink

Colony
8123 Harford Road
1949
John Zink

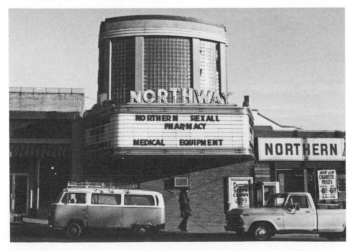

Northway
6701 Harford Road
1937
John Zink

Paramount
6650 Belair Road
1946
Hal Miller

Note: Personally, I enjoy seeing a movie at a theater like the Senator much more than at one of the newer "theaters" at a shopping center or mall. Theater, like architecture, is a total experience. The Deco movie houses were a perfect marriage of both experiences that should remain for us to enjoy in the future.—S.C.

Uptown
5010 Park Heights Avenue
1941
John Eyring

Westway
5300 Edmonson Avenue
1939
J.E. Moxley

Senator Theater
5904 York Road
1939
John Zink

The Senator Theater is an excellent showcase for the finish materials of the era. Glass block, neon, bakelite, and stainless steel are used throughout the exterior and interior.

Lobby, c. 1930

Bakelite
Exterior detail

Grand
509 South Conkling Street
1926
Architect unknown

Hollywood
Oregon Avenue
1934
Tunick Organization

Earle
4847 Belair Road
1937
John Eyring

Pikes
1001 Reisterstown Road
1937
John Eyring

BALTIMORE
DECO
1930
INSTITUTIONAL
BUILDINGS

Community Service Center,
Baltimore City Hospitals
Eastern Avenue
1931
E. Palmer, Architect

This building is constructed of light grey smooth brick with a concrete block base. The metal faceted windows are recessed in vertical brick piers and are separated by decorative metal panels. The overall design of the building consists of two side wings with an east-west axis running perpendicular to the main horizontal mass. The concrete two-story entrance features spectacular stainless steel and glass doors. Cornices and all classic detailing have been omitted and the overall appearance is modern and void of decoration. Entry to the building site is accented by two concrete gateways which have "Baltimore City Hospitals" engraved on them.

University Of Maryland Hospital
Redwood & Greene Streets
1934
Herbert G. Crisp,
James R. Edmunds, Jr.,
Wilson W. Smith,
Howard May, Architects

In the year in which work began on the new University of Maryland Hospital, Baltimore was in the midst of the Great Depression and construction of the building was heralded as an unemployment relief measure. The new building replaced the Baltimore Infirmary which was located half a block away, and had first opened in 1823.

The design for the hospital was unusual in that it was in the form of a cross of St. George—most hospitals were U- or H-shaped. Four wings radiate north, south, east, and west from the central tower, which houses the elevators and all noise making equipment, including ventilating machines. The wings, in which patient rooms and wards are located, were meant to provide maximum fresh air and sunlight.

The original plans called for a twelve-story building, but once construction started it was realized that there would not be enough funding to complete all floors, so only ten stories were finished. In 1938 work began on the final two floors. The building, made of red brick, was built in a series of set-backs. The central tower is topped by a wide stepped-in concrete band. The Greene Street entrance has two-story columns which frame the entry door; above this is a horizontal cornice embellished with carved Deco-style lettering. The Frank Bresser Research Laboratory and the School of Pharmacy—both of which are good examples of Baltimore Deco—are also located in the University medical complex.

**Administration Building,
Baltimore City Schools**
3 East 25th Street
1930
Lucius R. White, Architect

This granite-front structure has three-story fluting which frames the entry and is the center focus for metal casement windows and other Deco metal panels and trim. The overall building shape is defined by a geometric simplicity, yet the exterior molding has both geometric and waterfall-inspired themes that are quite elaborate and elegant. Brass double doors with geometric pulls are topped by a transom which is covered by elaborate Art Deco detail. The entry is flanked by bronze light fixtures in urn formation.
The interior is also quite elegant and features molding that echoes the exterior detail. The use of lavish finish materials—marble baseboard molding, maple columns, and bronze ceiling fixtures—adds to the overall sense of elegance.

Dunbar Middle School
Caroline Street
1931
Taylor & Fisher, Architects

The exterior of this castle-like structure is of multicolor brick. Solid squared-off vertical columns separate the bays, which contain four windows each. The windows are set in and are separated by narrow vertical piers which end in pointed finials. Cast concrete is used to form the various decorative details throughout. The entry is marked by an elegant brick and concrete turret. Solid vertical columns are used to separate the windows and the Deco arrowhead motif panels above the window levels.

Hampstead Hill Junior High School
101 South Ellwood Avenue
1933
Wyatt & Nolting, Architects

This red brick buiding uses black brick stripes to create the beautiful geometric patterns which are an integral part of the total design. Off-center towers create the vertical direction necessary to break up the horizontal massiveness of the structure. Continuous ribbons of red brick serve as important horizontal design elements. A two-story green stone entry is topped with a stepped-in parapet wall. The use of metal faceted windows further accents the play of one geometric form against the other.

Garrison Junior High School
3900 Barrington Road
1931
Smith & May, Architects

This school is constructed of red brick with cast concrete ornamental trim. The horizontal plan of the main building has two side wings with no openings. There are inset pattterns in stone bearing floral and geometric motifs. A central tower over the impressive entry accentuates the vertical elements in the design. Stepped-in finials on the side columns run the entire height of the building for further vertical interest.

Pump and Blower Station
Patapsco Sewage Plant
1940
Frank O. Heyder, Architect

This light orange brick building is still in use today. The stepped-in full height entry features a faceted window panel and lovely stainless steel lettering in Deco typeface. Solid vertical piers separate the window bays which are crowned by geometric brick panels for accent. The windows have stepped-in molding at either side for further geometric interest.

Fourier Library
College of Notre Dame
Homeland Avenue
1941
Frederick Vernon Murphy,
Architect

St. Katherine's Church
1222 North Luzerne Avenue
1933
Henry Dagit & Sons of
Philadelphia, Architects

St. Katherine's contains interior
craftsmanship of the highest level.
The mosaics were crafted by H.
Meire. The Deco-patterned terrazzo floors were designed and in-
stalled by Joseph Dunn & Sons,
while the stained glass was made
by Henry Lee Willett. The architect for the church designed the
furniture.

Associated Jewish Charities
319 West Monument Street
1939
B. Frank, Architect

This red brick corner building has a vertical emphasis centering on the entryway. A stepped-in door pediment runs the full height of the building and there are flat grooved columns on either side of the door. At the corners of the structure are solid red brick piers. Horizontal rhythm is set by the continuous concrete ribbon across the top and on either side of the entry structure. The green veined marble panels used to separate the window levels also convey horizontal interest.

Enoch Pratt Free Library
400 Cathedral Street
1933
Clyde N. Friz, Architect

Interior detail

U.S. Appraisers Stores
Lombard & Gay Streets
1935
Taylor & Fisher,
William F. Stone, Jr., Architects

This building was built on the site
of the previous U.S. Appraisers
Stores which was destroyed by
fire. The cost of the second
building was $900,000 and it
boasted "fireproof construction."
The brick and granite structure has
a solid, massive appearance, yet
the strong geometric elements
successfully redefine the mass so
that it does not appear bulky. The
windows are set between solid
vertical piers which emphasize the
strong vertical design elements. A
two-story granite foundation incorporates flat vertical columns
which frame the entry. Especially
notable are the top cutaway corners of the building which are
composed of Deco stylized eagles,
complete with vertical ribbing on
the wings.

BALTIMORE
DECO
RESIDENCES

Samester Apartments
7000 Park Heights Avenue
1936
Hal A. Miller, Architect

The Samester Apartments consist
of a cluster of buildings arranged in
a zig-zag pattern built around a
central landscaped area. The
Apartments were the first
FHA-207 job in the United States
and won many design awards
when built. The low-rise buildings
are constucted of red brick with
black glazed brick used to create a
pattern. The structure has steel
double-hung windows. An entry
consisting of a stainless steel
canopy with metal and opal glass
geometric fixtures is placed in the
central tower of each building.
Bullet-shaped concrete and black
brick columns frame glass block
stripes on either side of the door-
ways. The light fixtures on the
property are bronze variations of
torcheres with inverted shades.

Soderstrom Residence
300 Northfield Place
1947
S. Shackelford, Architect

The Soderstrom residence is a one and one-half story structure with a painted stucco exterior. It consists of cube-like masses with a metal-railed terrace which provides a strong visual element for the front facade. The use of steel casement windows provides a wraparound effect on the corners of the house; ribbon windows give a vertical accent.

Residence
333-335 Belvedere Avenue
1939
Palmer & Lamdin, Architects

Unique to the neighborhood, this brick and glass block structure is surrounded by Colonial style homes. A flat, curved canopy covers the entry area. Steel casement windows are accented by wraparound brick stripes at each corner. The lack of traditional exterior trim enhances this simple yet elegant residential building.

Residence
2105 Erdman Avenue
1945
B.N. Eisenberg, Designer & Builder

This is a sculptural stucco
residence with molding stripes
following the curved design. The
various uses of windows are
especially important in the design
scheme. There are wraparound
windows at the curves and at the
corners. Ribbon windows are used
to accent the horizontal flow and
are fitted between the molding
stripes. There is a continuous
overhang which wraps around the
building and whose line is mirrored
by a stone planter at ground level.
A sleek look results from the
general absence of trim and traditional molding.

Residence
3707 St. Paul Street
1937
John Ahlers, Architect

This two-story white brick structure has a low roof line which accents the box-like architectural
design. Continuous ribbon molding
between floor levels is broken by
vertical accents at the corners of
the structure. Brick is used in a
strong geometric pattern as accent, with triangular and stepping-
back design elements. The windows are wood casement and
there is glass block used in the
front and rear entries.

BALTIMORE
DECO

SIGNAGE

Signs convey a company's image and are geared toward attracting attention. During the Deco years, new materials and methods were incorporated into the art of signage and many excellent examples remain today. Etched glass and stone, bold electric bulb signs, as well as elaborate free-hanging neon, were all used effectively. Stainless steel lettering was proudly applied to Deco exteriors. Colored enamelled panels were embellished with Deco-style lettering. The typefaces typical of the period were relatively plain, sometimes with varying line weights. Generally, the lettering had the same qualities as the architecture—it was simple, angular, geometric, yet elegant.

<u>First Column</u>

China Clipper
1003 North Charles Street
Neon

Macgillivray's Pharmacy
900 North Charles Street
Paint on Metal

Patapsco Sewage Plant
Stainless Steel Letters

White Rice Inn
320 Park Avenue
Neon

<u>Second Column</u>

The 2 O'Clock Club
Baltimore Street
Flashing Neon

Van Dyke & Bacon
5851 York Road
Neon

People's Liquor
20 North Howard Street
Neon
(Note: Sign removed in 1982)

<u>Third Column</u>

Charles Fish & Sons
Eutaw & Franklin Streets
Etched Black Glass

United Sanitary Chemical
1901 North Howard Street
Flashing Neon

Buck Appliance Company
1800 Fleet Street
Paint on Metal

Belair Market
Stainless Steel Letters

Ambassador Beauty Salon
39th Street & Canterbury Road
Etched Glass, Wood

Patterson Theater
3136 Eastern Avenue
Bulb Lights

New China Inn
2430 North Charles Street
Neon
(Note: Sign removed in 1983.)

Kaymar Beauty Salon
5204 Leeds Avenue
Stainless Steel, Neon

BALTIMORE
DECO

ARCHITECTS &
WALKING TOUR

The following are brief biographies of architects who designed extensively in the Baltimore area (although not always in the Deco mode). Each did at least one Deco building, and some did many more. Almost all were born in Baltimore in the last century; none are living today. All of their designs, whether monumental or residential, form a priceless legacy which the city of Baltimore should value and maintain, whether through renovation or preservation. A lost heritage can never be reclaimed.

—Mary R. Cowgill

James R. Edmunds, Jr. was born in Baltimore in 1890. After graduating from the University of Pennsylvania he worked for Palmer, Wyatt & Nolting. In 1920 he joined Joseph Sperry, and in 1923 became a partner in the firm. During the years 1923-28 Edmunds was the Baltimore correspondent for the Beaux Arts Institute of Design in Paris. In 1930 he established the firm Crisp & Edmunds.

Edmunds was a registered architect in eight states and an honorary member of the Royal Institute of British Architects. He was nationally known for his excellent hospital designs. In Baltimore he designed Union Memorial, was the consulting architect for University Hospital, designed Hutzler's on Howard Street, Hutzler's in Towson, Hochschild Kohn's Belvedere, and Hochschild's Service Center downtown. Edmunds also modernized the facades of the original Hutzler's on Howard Street and the Hochschild Kohn store in the same block. In addition to department stores, Edmunds designed Eastern and Western High Schools in Baltimore. He also lived in Canton, China for several years and designed fifteen schools and public buildings there. Some of the hospitals he designed in the United States were located in Lancaster, Pennsylvania; Knoxville, Tennessee; Greenville, South Carolina; and Tallahassee, Florida.

In 1945, Edmunds was elected president of the American Institute of Architects. That same year, Frank Lloyd Wright issued a scathing attack on the AIA and Edmunds. Edmunds rebutted by calling Wright the ''P.T. Barnum of architecture—a very capable architect but completely intolerant of any views other than his own.'' Edmunds later became head of the AIA committee which studied the effects of atomic energy on design. He also fought against the membership limitations of the AIA, contending that the organization should be open to all who qualified and not just a select few.

J.F. Eyring was the son of Erhard Eyring, a builder and contractor who headed the firm E. Eyring & Sons, Co. (1887). J.F. Eyring started his own firm in 1927 and concentrated on the design and building of schools, churches, and commercial and industrial buildings. He was a member of AIA. His designs include the Mt. St. Agnes College Library; St. Dominic's Church; the First National Bank at 3401 Eastern Avenue (1940); the Earle Theater, Belair Road (1937); the Uptown Theater, Park Heights Avenue (1941); and the Pikes Theater, Reisterstown Road (1937).

Hal A. Miller was born in Montreal, Canada, but became a naturalized citizen in 1930. He attended McGill University and graduated with a degree in architecture. Miller also took courses in apartment house planning at Columbia University. In 1936, he opened an independent firm at 421 St. Paul Place. In 1938, Jerome Kahn became a partner, but in 1939 this connection was discontinued.

Miller specialized in what was called ''modernistic'' design. His apartment buildings were known as ''thoroughly up-to-date'' and modern. He designed and built the Dunmanway apartments in Dundalk; the Samester-Parkway apartments, which received the Chamber of Commerce award because of outstanding design; the Claymont apartments in Claymont, Maryland; the Dunmore apartments in Dundalk; the Ramblewood complex; Suburban Park and the Park Central apartments in Baltimore. Miller at one time lived in the Samester-Parkway apartments.

Miller also designed the General Vending Sales Corporation on Biddle Street; the Paramount Theater on Belair Road (1946); and the WBAL transmitting station. He was a charter member of the Maryland Society of Architects.

Frederick Vernon Murphy was born in Fond du Lac, Wisconsin in 1879. He studies at l'Ecole des Beaux Arts, Paris and was an AIA member. Murphy specialized in church design and designed many churches in several states. In Baltimore he designed the Fourier Library of the College of Notre Dame on Charles Street. Murphy was a consulting architect for the National Shrine of the Immaculate Conception. He was awarded a gold medal for design for the Sacred Heart Church in Washington, D.C. and the John Kenneth Mullen Library, also in D.C.

William G. Nolting was born in Baltimore in 1866. He established the firm of Wyatt & Nolting in the latter part of the last century and he and Wyatt remained associates for more than thirty years. Their practice has been recognized as one of Baltimore's most talented architectural firms. They were responsible for the design of the Baltimore Court House at Calvert and Fayette Streets, the Keyser Building at Redwood and Calvert Streets, the original Roland Park Country Club, the old Patterson Park High School (1933) at Pratt and Ellwood Streets (which has been called reminiscent of the Bauhaus), and the 5th Regiment Armory.

Edward Livingston Palmer was born in Baltimore in 1888. Palmer was a pioneer architect in the field of controlled development and it was he who helped set the pattern for Roland Park, Guilford, Homeland, and other exclusive residential areas of Baltimore City.

In the 1930s Palmer formed a partnership with William D. Lamdin and for more than half a century their firm designed many architectural landmarks in Baltimore. City Hospitals on Eastern Avenue was originally known as the Bay View Asylum. In the late 1920s Palmer surveyed the conditions and physical facilities there, and recommended changes for rehabilitation and expansion. On the basis of his report the city transformed a neglected and inefficient 'almshouse' into a modern medical center for the people of Baltimore—the City Hospitals. In 1932, Palmer and Lamdin designed the Nurses' Home and Gateway for the hospital.

1020 St. Paul Street is the office building that Palmer and Lamdin designed in 1938 to house their architectural firm. Palmer also designed the present Sunpapers building on Calvert Street (1952) and the Guilford house which was the Decorator Showhouse for 1983.

William D. Lamdin, also a Baltimore native, was born in 1883. Lamdin was a fellow of the AIA and a graduate of the Cornell School of Architecture.

John Poe Tyler was yet another Baltimore native, born in 1907. He was a descendant of President John Tyler and Edgar Allan Poe. Tyler graduated from Princeton University in 1929 with a B.S. in architecture. He became an associate of Joseph Evans Sperry after graduating and in 1936 began practicing independently. One of the first designs he worked on was the Edgar Allan Poe housing project. He also assisted in the work on the State House in St. Mary's City. The popular night club, The Hippo, on North Charles Street was designed by Tyler in 1939.

Lucius Read White, Jr. was born in Baltimore in 1887. He was a graduate of Baltimore City College and studied architecture at the University of Pennsylvania. In 1922 he established an independent practice and in 1949 took his son, Edward G. White, into the firm. White designed jails, housing projects, hospitals, and churches, as well as educational, commercial, and industrial buildings.

Some of the buildings that White designed are: the Court Square Building; the Administration Building, Baltimore City Schools; Bachrach Studios; Greyhound Bus Terminal (associate); Crown Cork and Seal Co., Inc.; Federal Housing Projects, Baltimore; New Baltimore City Jail; Gymnasium and Library, Loyola College; Ashburton Filtration Plant (consultant); the Greenspring Dairy; and Fiske Catering (originally Heidelbach Co.).

John J. Zink, a Baltimore native, was born in 1886. Zink was a graduate of the Maryland Institute. He worked in Baltimore and New York and was primarily interested in designing theaters. Zink was a member of the firm Zink, Atkins, and Craycroft and a member of the AIA. Before his death in 1952, John Zink had designed over 200 theaters. Some of the Baltimore area theaters are the Ambassador, Liberty Heights Avenue (1935); the Colony, Harford Road (1949); the Northway, Harford Road (1937); and the Deco crown jewel—the Senator, York Road (1939).

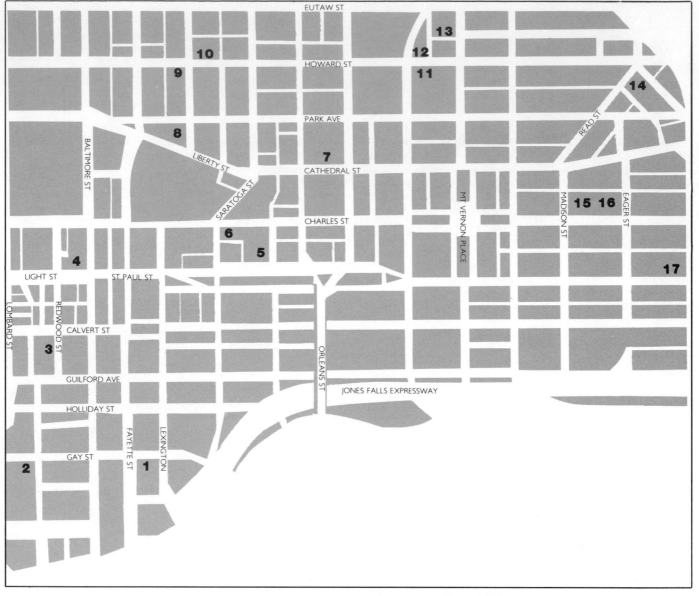

(Page numbers in parentheses)

1. War Memorial (Cover)
2. United States Appraisers Stores (48)
3. Werner's Restaurant (23)
4. Maryland National Bank (12)
5. C&P Telephone Company (17)
6. Commercial Credit Company (16)
7. Enoch Pratt Free Library (47)
8. Kresge's 5 & 10 (20)
9. Read's Drug Store (21)
10. Hutzler's Department Store (8)

11. Greyhound Bus Terminal (32)
12. White Tower Restaurant (28)
13. Associated Jewish Charities (47)
14. General Vending Sales Corporation (30)
15. Commercial Building, 930 N. Charles St. (19)
16. Hippo Nightclub (26)
17. Commercial Building, 1020 St. Paul St. (19)

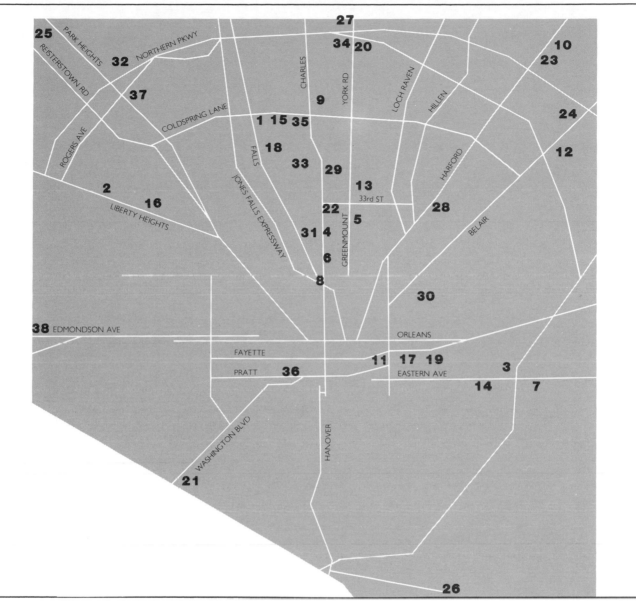

John Kardys: Pages 9 (top, bottom left), 10, 13, 14, 15, 16 (top left, bottom), 17 (left), 23, 24 (top, center, bottom right), 26 (top), 30, 31 (top, bottom left), 37 (bottom right), 42 (top right, bottom center), 46, 56 (top left), 64.

Larry Goldberg: Pages 20 (bottom), 40 (top)

Maxwell MacKenzie: Cover, Title Page, Page 26 (bottom).

Colin Varga: Page 36 (top, center right).

Courtesy Jacques Kelly: Pages 8, 12, 21 (top), 32 (top), 41, 48.

Courtesy Durkee Enterprises: Pages 20 (top), 36 (bottom), 37 (top, bottom left).

Courtesy Hutzler's: Page 11.

Courtesy Enoch Pratt Free Library: Page 47 (bottom)

Reprinted from **Design Action** (September/October 1982): Maps, Pages 60, 61.

All Other Photographs by the Author.

Battersby, Martin. **The Decorative Twenties.** New York: Walker and Company, 1969.

Battersby, Martin. **The Decorative Thirties.** New York: Walker and Company, 1971.

Brown, Robert. **Art Deco Internationale.** New York: Quick Fox, 1977.

Capitman, Barbara, Editor. **Portfolio, Art Deco Historic District.** Miami Beach: Bucolo Preservation Press, 1979.

Cerwinske, Laura. **Tropical Deco.** New York: Rizzoli International, 1981.

Dorsey, John, and James D. Dilts. **A Guide to Baltimore Architecture.** Centreville, Md.: Tidewater Publishers, 1981.

Grief, Martin, **Depression Modern.** New York: Universe Books, 1975.

Headley, Robert, Jr. **Exit.** University Park, Md.: Robert Headley, Jr., 1974.

Hirshorn, Paul, and Steven Izenour. **White Towers.** Cambridge, Mass.: The MIT Press, 1981.

Kummer, Frederic Arnold, C.E., and Ferdinand C. Latrobe. **The Free State of Maryland.** Baltimore: The Historical Record Association, N.D.

Notter, Anderson, Finegold, Inc. **Miami Beach Art Deco District—Preservation and Development Plan.** Boston: 1981.

Records of the Maryland Historical Trust.

Sunpapers obituary files.

Walters, Thomas. **Art Deco.** Great Britain: Academy Editions, 1973.

I decided to do this survey for two reasons: first to fulfill a requirement for my degree in Interior Design from the Maryland Institute of Art, which I received in May 1982; also to satisfy my own fascination with and dedication to Art Deco. This has been more than a passing interest for me. I have searched out Deco items in thrift shops and flea markets, whether working or on vacation, in every city I've visited for the past ten years. Currently I am a member of the Miami Design Preservation League and the New York Art Deco Society, and I visit both cities regularly to observe the progress of these groups. I have found that interior design is a perfect outlet for the Deco ideas I have stored in my head; and I have tried to incorporate the various themes and principles of Deco design into my work. Retromodern, of which I am a principal, specializes in architecture and interior design influenced by the 1920s, 30s, 40s, and 50s.

We recreated the ambiance of a Deco dinette (complete with glass block and a Wurlitzer) at the 1982 Baltimore Symphony Showhouse. My first published work, a walking and touring map of Baltimore's Art Deco, appeared in **Design Action**.

When I was awarded a grant from the National Endowment for the Arts, it was a perfect opportunity to take the first steps in paving the way for Art Deco preservation in Baltimore. This book has also helped to bring about the birth of the Baltimore Deco Society, of which I am currently president. In doing my research I met many people who were eager to aid me and who also appreciate Baltimore Deco. Hopefully, our city's significant Deco buildings will be saved and preserved for future enjoyment.